MODERN OLYMPICS

HAYDN MIDDLETON

Heinemann
LIBRARY

www.heinemann.co.uk/library

Visit our website to find out more information about **Heinemann Library** books.

To order:

☎ Phone 44 (0) 1865 888066

📄 Send a fax to 44 (0) 1865 314091

💻 Visit the Heinemann bookshop at www.heinemann.co.uk/library to browse our catalogue and order online.

First published in Great Britain by Heinemann Library, Halley Court, Jordan Hill, Oxford OX2 8EJ,
part of Harcourt Education.

Heinemann is a registered trademark of Harcourt Education Ltd.

Editorial: Nicole Irving and Georga Godwin.
Design: Ticktock Media and Tim Bones.
Production: Viv Hichens.

Originated by Ambassador Litho Ltd
Printed and bound in China by South China Printing Company

ISBN 0 431 18427 5 (hardback)   ISBN 0 431 18430 5 (paperback)
07 06 05 04   08 07 06 05 04
10 9 8 7 6 5 4 3 2   10 9 8 7 6 5 4 3 2 1

Acknowledgements

The Publishers would like to thank the following for permission to reproduce photographs:

Ancient Art and Architecture: 5t. Corbis: 4t, 11t, 22r.
Empics: OFC, OBC, 4-5b, 6-7, 8-9, 10b, 11b, 12-13, 14-15,
16, 18-19, 20-21, 22t, 23t, 24-25, 26-27.

British Library Cataloguing in Publication Data
Author, Haydn Middleton
The Olympics - Modern Olympics

796.4'8
A full catalogue record for this book is available from the British Library.

CONTENTS

THE GAMES ARE BACK   4

THREE KINDS OF GAMES   6

SYMBOLS OF THE GAMES   8

THE HOST CITY   10

BEHIND THE SCENES   12

OLYMPIC TRACK EVENTS   14

OLYMPIC FIELD EVENTS   16

OLYMPIC WATER SPORTS   18

OLYMPIC TEAM SPORTS   20

OLYMPIC GYMNASTICS   22

OLYMPIC POWER AND PRECISION   24

TRUE OLYMPIC SPIRIT   26

OLYMPIC TIME LINE   28

GLOSSARY   30

INDEX   32

Any words appearing in the text in bold, **like this**, are explained in the Glossary.

THE GAMES ARE BACK

*Baron Pierre de Coubertin (second from left), father of the modern Olympics, pictured with the rest of the first International Olympic Committee (**IOC**).*

In April 1896 a huge sporting festival was held in Athens, Greece. It was called the Olympic Games. Over 300 men from fourteen different countries raced and jumped against one another. Vast crowds gathered to watch 43 different events. This 10-day festival took a lot of organizing. The man behind the event was a sport-loving Frenchman, Baron Pierre de Coubertin. The world's peoples often fought one another in wars, and de Coubertin wanted them instead to compete in peace for sporting glory. Since 1896 the Olympics have been held in seventeen different countries on four different continents and they remain the most important international athletic competition in the world. In 1997, Athens won the right to bring the Olympics home to Greece in 2004.

GREAT OLYMPIC EVENTS

The marathon

The longest Olympic foot race is the marathon. Runners have to complete a course that is approximately 42.8 kilometres (26.8 miles) long. Despite the fact that there was no marathon in the ancient Olympics (the longest race then was just 4614 metres), the event is named after a great Greek victory over Persian invaders in 490 BC. According to a later legend, a Greek messenger ran all the way from a place called Marathon to Athens – approximately 40 kilometres (26 miles) – with the joyful news, then dropped dead!

The Athens Games of 1896 were not the first Olympics. Those were held almost 3000 years ago. From 776 **BC** until **AD** 393, athletes from all over the Greek world came to a place called Olympia every four years to compete in a five-day athletics event called the Olympic Games. That was where de Coubertin got the idea for the modern Games.

This painting on a Greek vase made in the 4th century BC shows a chariot race. These were the most spectacular events at the ancient Olympic Games.

THEN & NOW
Men only?

Events at the ancient Olympics included chariot-racing and a race that involved running in armour. Only men were allowed to compete, and women were not even allowed to watch! The Games were part of a religious festival, held in honour of the Greek god Zeus. However, the modern Olympics are not religious in any way, and since 1900 women have been taking part, although they only began to compete in **track** *and* **field events** *after 1928.*

WORDS TO REMEMBER

'The most important thing in the Olympic Games is not to win but to take part, just as the most important thing in life is not the triumph but the struggle.' De Coubertin's words continue to reflect the true spirit of the Olympics. For those who do win, however, even today there are no financial rewards, although Olympic champions may receive cash from endorsements and advertising deals. For many years, only **amateur** *athletes were allowed to take part. Then one sport after another let* **professional** *athletes compete.*

The Ethiopian Abebe Bikila on his way to victory in the marathon at the 1960 Games in Rome, Italy.

THREE KINDS OF GAMES

The Jamaican Bobsleigh team at the 1998 Winter Olympics in Nagano, Japan.

Since 1896 the Olympics have been held every four years. They have only been cancelled three times: in 1916, 1940 and 1944, during World War I and World War II. Sometimes these Games are called the Summer Olympics. That is because, since 1924, there has been a separate Winter Olympic Games. Instead of competing at summer events like running, jumping and ball sports, athletes at the Winter Games skate, ski, snowboard and play ice hockey. Fewer countries send teams to these Games, because it is not easy to become a great skier or skater in places with warm climates and few mountains. But if you have enough talent, you can take part in the Games wherever you come from. At the 1992 Winter Games in Albertsville, France, there was even a four-man bobsleigh team from the hot West Indian island of Jamaica.

WORDS TO REMEMBER

The Olympic motto is made up of three Latin words: citius, altius and fortius. They mean swifter, higher and stronger. Each Summer, Winter and Paralympic athlete aims to perform better than all the others. The best-ever performance in each event is described as an Olympic record.

Korea and Peru compete in a volleyball match at the 2000 Games in Sydney, Australia.

GREAT OLYMPIC EVENTS

Connie Hansen

At the 1988 Paralympic Games in Seoul, South Korea, Denmark's wheelchair athlete Connie Hansen hit the headlines by winning no fewer than five events. She came home first in the 400 metres, 800 metres, 1500 metres, 5000 metres and wheelchair marathon races. Then at the 1992 Paralympics in Barcelona, Spain, Hansen won the marathon again!

Wheelchair athletes compete in the tennis event at the 2000 Paralympics in Sydney.

Since 1960 there has been a third kind of Olympics for athletes with disabilities. These games are called the Paralympics, and they take place every four years around the same time as the Summer Olympics. In 1960, 400 disabled men and women took part in the first Paralympics in Rome. Forty years later, ten times as many athletes were competing at the Paralympics in Sydney at all sorts of sports from basketball to rhythmic gymnastics. This book will give you some information on the Winter Olympics and Paralympics, but it is mainly about the Summer Games.

THEN & NOW

When are the Winter Games?

At the first Summer Games there were some winter sports like figure-skating and ice hockey. Then in 1924, at Chamonix in France, the first Winter Games were held. In that year the French also held the Summer Olympics in Paris. Until 1992 the Winter and Summer Games were always held in the same year, although not always in the same country. Since 1994, however, the Winter Games have taken place two years after each Summer Games. The 2002 Winter Games were held at Salt Lake City, USA, with nearly 2400 athletes taking part in 78 events.

SYMBOLS OF THE GAMES

The Olympic torch is lit at the 2000 Games in Sydney.

The Games are always great to watch, whether you are a spectator in the Olympic stadium or part of the world-wide TV audience. They open and close with spectacular ceremonies. At the Games' opening, all the competitors march past, with the team from Greece in front, followed by those from all the other countries in alphabetical order. From 1928 onwards, the organizers of the Games started a custom of lighting a flame in the Olympic stadiums. Since 1936 this flame has been brought from Olympia in Greece, where the ancient Games were held. Usually it is carried by torch-bearers, but in 1976, a hot beam of light was sent from Olympia to light a torch in faraway Montreal, Canada.

WORDS TO REMEMBER

At the start of each Games since 1920, an athlete takes the Olympic oath on behalf of all the other competitors from around the world. 'I promise,' he or she says, 'that we will take part in these Olympic Games, respecting the rules which govern them, in the true spirit of sportsmanship, for the glory of sport and the honour of our teams.'

STRANGE BUT TRUE

An unforgettable opening

When the 1984 Games were held in Los Angeles, USA, the opening ceremony was stunning. Ninety thousand spectators – plus hundreds of millions of TV viewers – watched a magnificent spectacle lasting four and a half hours. It featured over 10,000 performers, including a jet-propelled rocket man who flew through the air before landing in the Olympic stadium, the Coliseum.

The spectacular opening ceremony for the 2000 Sydney Olympics.

At the closing ceremony the flame is put out, and the five-ringed Olympic flag is taken down. It is then handed over to the city that will stage the next Games. The flag was designed by Baron de Coubertin, and has flown at every Games since those at Antwerp, Belgium in 1920. Back then, the flags of all nations could be made up from its five colours and white background. Today the rings stand for the world's five continents, which are linked together by the playing of Olympic sport.

Sweden's Lars Froelander (centre) celebrates his gold medal along with Australian silver-medallist Michael Klim (left) and Australian bronze-medallist Geoff Huegill (right) in the men's 100 metres butterfly swimming final at the 2000 Games in Sydney.

THE HOST CITY

The city where each Games is held is called the host city. The host city for the first modern Olympics was Athens, Greece, in 1896. Over a century later, the city won the right to host the 28th Games in 2004. Keen sports fans have sometimes asked for every Games to be held there, since Greece is the birthplace of Olympic sport. But because the modern Olympics are now truly **global** festivals, they have been staged in great cities all over the world.

GREAT OLYMPIANS

Olympic Mascots

Since 1972 one or more official mascots have become known throughout the world as symbols of fun at each Olympic festival. The first mascot was Waldi the Dachshund, a dog who appeared at the 1972 Munich Games. At the 2000 Games in Sydney, there were three mascots – Ollie the kookaburra, Syd the platypus and Millie the Echidna.

THEN & NOW

Who pays for the Olympics?

*It costs a lot of money to host an Olympics, and the Games are getting more expensive all the time. In 1936 the German government had to pay approximately £19 million, raised through **taxes**, to stage the Games in Berlin. In 1972, when the Games were held in Germany again in Munich, it cost almost 70 times that amount. The 1976 Games in Montreal, Canada, were so dear that Canadian taxpayers took twenty years to cover the cost! Today commercial **sponsors** like Coca-Cola help to cover the cost. In 1996, companies paid a total of £126 million to sponsor the Atlanta Games in the USA. Money is also raised from making TV companies pay huge sums for the rights to show Olympic events.*

This character is called Misha the Bear, and was the mascot for the 1980 Games in Moscow, Russia.

SWIFTER, HIGHER, STRONGER ... FAIRER?

Today there is always fierce competition to host the Olympic Games. Bidders from some cities are so keen to win, they cheat. In 1999 a scandal broke when it was proved that several cities had bribed IOC officials to vote for their bids. There was another bribe scandal in the bidding for the 2002 Winter Games. It was alleged that officials from the successful American city, Utah, had given gifts to members of the IOC.

A poster from the 1936 Olympic Games.

The current president of the IOC, Jacques Rogge.

The **IOC** decides which city will host the Games. To be chosen as a host city is a great honour, so several cities usually put in a **bid**. Eleven cities, including Cape Town, Rio de Janeiro and Istanbul, put in bids for the 2004 Games. The IOC officials choose the city they believe will be the best host to all the athletes and spectators. They make their decision a long time before the Games, so that the host city can make all its preparations. In 1993, Sydney was chosen to hold the 27th Games, which were not due to take place until 2000!

BEHIND THE SCENES

Each modern Games lasts for around two weeks. The host city and Olympic officials spend years making sure everything will run smoothly. This is no simple task, because they have to deal with huge numbers of visitors. For the 1996 Games in Atlanta, USA, eleven million entrance tickets were on offer. All these spectators could

The Olympic Stadium in Athens, Greece.

watch different sports at 21 **venues** in and around the city. To get them there on time each day, the city's transport had to be working very efficiently. That is why the organizers called these Games 'the largest peacetime ... event in human history'.

THEN AND NOW

At the 1996 Games in Atlanta, it cost over £125 million just to pay for security. Despite this expense, however, terrorists managed to plant a bomb that killed one person and injured 110 others. The worst atrocity in Olympic history, however, took place at the Munich Games in 1972. Terrorists broke into the Olympic Village there, and eleven athletes from Israel were killed. A total of 50,000 guards have been hired to patrol the 2004 Games in Athens. Greece has received guarantees of security assistance from 37 other countries.

The Olympic flag flies at half-mast to commemorate those who died at the 1972 Games in Munich. Today, host countries employ tens of thousands of security guards to try to prevent such an attack from happening again.

The Canadian sprinter Ben Johnson, who was caught taking drugs at the 1988 Games in Seoul, South Korea. He was stripped of his 100 metres gold medal and banned from competing for several years.

GREAT OLYMPIANS

THE VOLUNTEERS

No modern Games could take place without volunteer helpers. For no reward except a share in the fun of the Olympics, 46,967 of them were busily at work at the 2000 Games in Sydney. An amazing 60,000 volunteers have signed up to help at the Athens Games in 2004. Anyone over eighteen years old can help, and volunteers come from countries all over the world. The jobs they do include keeping the venues clean, providing food and transport and attending to the many needs of athletes, officials and spectators.

A host city also has to provide accommodation for athletes and officials. For the 1920 Games in Antwerp, Belgium, the competitors stayed in the city's schools, eight sleeping in each classroom! At the Los Angeles Games of 1932, a new tradition began. A special Olympic village was built for the male athletes to live in, complete with its own fire station, post office and hospital. There were only 127 women athletes, so they stayed in a Los Angeles hotel. Later Olympic villages have been built on unused land. When the Games are over, local people can then move into the apartments.

OLYMPIC TRACK EVENTS

The wheelchair athlete
Tanni Grey-Thomson,
winner of nine gold medals
at the Paralympics.

Track events are some of the most thrilling at any Olympic Games. Races like the men's 100 metres, 400 metres and 1500 metres have featured since the first modern Games at Athens in 1896. Others, like the 20,000 metres walk, were added later. Some of the best known Olympians of all time were track athletes. The wonderful long-distance runner Emil Zatopek of Czechoslovakia won three gold medals in eight days at the 1952 Games in Helsinki. Sprinter Fanny Blankers-Koen, known as the Dutch Flying Housewife, won four at the 1948 Games in London. More recently at the 1996 Games in Atlanta, the USA's Michael Johnson became the first man ever to win gold in both the 200 metres and 400 metres. Four years later, he won the 400 metres again at the 2000 Olympics in Sydney.

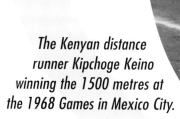

The Kenyan distance
runner Kipchoge Keino
winning the 1500 metres at
the 1968 Games in Mexico City.

SWIFTER, HIGHER, STRONGER

100 metres records through the ages

Date	Record holder	Time (secs)
1896	Thomas Burke (USA)	12.0
1924	Harold Abrahams (Britain)	10.6
1936	Jesse Owens (USA)	10.3
1960	Armin Hary (Germany)	10.2
1964	Robert Hayes (USA)	10.05
1968	James Hines (USA)	9.95
1988	Carl Lewis (USA)	9.92
1996	Donovan Bailey (Canada)	9.84

For athletes aiming to break Olympic or world records, timing is vital. At the earlier Games, officials timed runners and walkers with simple stopwatches. Since 1932, however, more accurate electronic timing has been used. Instruments called anemometers are also used to measure wind speeds for shorter races. If an athlete is going to set an official record, the wind speed behind him or her must be less than two metres per second.

GREAT OLYMPIC EVENTS
Cross-country racing

At the Games of 1912, 1920 and 1924 there was a tough cross-country race. The last one, over a distance of about 10,000 metres, was a disaster. On a very hot Paris afternoon 38 runners set off but only fifteen finished. The course included stone paths covered in knee-high thistles and weeds. There was also a power station nearby, filling the air with poisonous fumes. Many runners pulled out with sunstroke and sickness. Hours after Paavo Nurmi of Finland won the gold medal, officials were still searching for missing runners by the roadsides. Since this disaster, there have been no more Olympic cross-country races.

THEN & NOW
Women athletes

Until the 1928 Games in Amsterdam, no women were allowed to compete in Olympic track and **field events**. Some people still believed women's bodies were too delicate for any race longer than 200 metres. After the 800 metres final in 1928, several runners collapsed. Doctors said women would 'become old too soon' if they kept running such distances, and the race was not held again until the 1960 Games. The 1500 metres for women became a regular Olympic event in 1972, followed in 1984 by the women's marathon.

The Ethiopian runner Derartu Tulu celebrates victory in the 10,000 metres at the 1992 Games in Barcelona, Spain.

OLYMPIC FIELD EVENTS

Like most **track events**, **field events** – which involve jumping and throwing – take place inside the Olympic stadium. Some, like the discus, date back to ancient Olympic times. Others have been introduced more recently. The women's pole vault, for example, appeared for the first time at the 2000 Games in Sydney. Huge stadium crowds have watched not only fantastic individual field performances, but also some breathtaking jumping and throwing contests between the world's greatest athletes.

The Czech javelin thrower Dana Zatopkova on her way to victory in the 1952 Games in Helsinki.

The British athlete Daley Thomson, winner of Olympic gold medals in the **decathlon** at the 1980 Games in Moscow and the 1984 Games in Los Angeles.

GREAT OLYMPIANS

Ray Ewry

Over 100 years before the Paralympics began, American Ray Ewry fell ill with a disease called polio. Put in a wheelchair, he was told he might be paralysed for life. Ewry, however, began to exercize on his own, and he not only walked again, but jumped into Olympic history. Between 1900 and 1908 he won a total of eight gold medals in the standing high jump, standing long jump and standing triple jump. These events were dropped from the Games in 1912, but memories of Ewry's magnificent achievement will last forever.

THEN & NOW

The Javelin

Athletes can throw the javelin much further than the shot, discus or hammer. So far, in fact, that in 1986 the grip of the men's javelin was moved up by 10 centimetres and its tail was made more narrow. This made it fly for shorter distances when thrown. Officials were worried that otherwise runners on the track or even spectators on the far side of the stadium might be hit by the metal-tipped missiles!

In an amazing triple jump competition at the 1972 Games in Munich, the old world record was beaten nine times. Russia's Viktor Saneyev finally clinched victory with a gigantic hop, step and jump of 17.39 metres. That same year, Germany's Ulrike Meyfarth cleared 1.92 metres to win the women's high jump. Aged just sixteen, she was the youngest ever individual gold-medallist in an Olympic field event. Four years earlier, at the 1968 Games in Mexico City, Bob Beamon of the USA changed long jump history when he leapt a massive 8.90 metres – breaking the world record by 55 centimetres. He was so surprised that his legs buckled beneath him afterwards, but his new record stood until 1991.

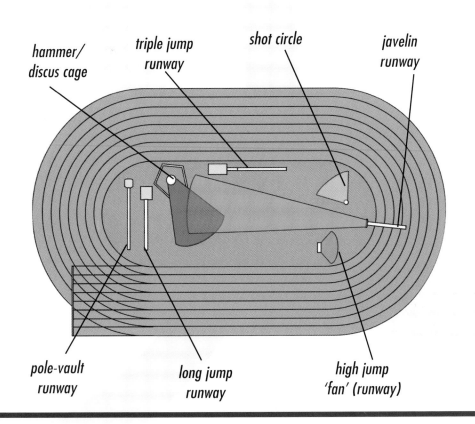

hammer/ discus cage

triple jump runway

shot circle

javelin runway

pole-vault runway

long jump runway

high jump 'fan' (runway)

SWIFTER, HIGHER, STRONGER

Better poles, higher vaults

*Olympic vaulters have made huge progress as their poles became more flexible. At the earliest Games they used heavy wooden poles. Then around 1912, poles of bamboo came in, to be replaced by **aluminium** in the 1950s, then by **fibreglass** after 1960. As a result of these changes, the world record for the pole vault has increased from 3.30 metres in 1896 to 5.92 metres in 1996.*

OLYMPIC WATER SPORTS

GREAT OLYMPIC EVENTS

Wonderkids

Marjorie Gestring of the USA is the youngest ever individual gold-medal winner at the Olympics. Aged thirteen and three-quarters, she won the springboard diving competition at the 1936 Games in Berlin. But she may not be the youngest ever Olympian. At the 1900 Games in Paris, a small French boy was chosen to be **cox** of a Dutch rowing team that won the gold medal. His name is now unknown, and so was his age at the time, but some eye-witnesses believed he was as young as seven!

The first Olympic swimming contests were held outdoors in the icy Bay of Zea at the 1896 Games in Athens. Two of the three races were won by 18-year-old Alfred Hajos of Hungary, whose father had drowned five years earlier.

Since 1896, a host of fine athletes have thrilled Olympic crowds from the water – not just swimmers and divers, but yachtsmen and women, canoeists and rowers too.

The diver Sun Shuwei on his way to a gold medal for platform diving at the 1992 Games in Barcelona.

The Australian Dawn Fraser, who won four gold and four silver medals in Olympic swimming events.

STRANGE BUT TRUE

From fast lanes to films

Four Olympic medallists went into the movies to play the role of Tarzan, a popular action hero brought up by apes in the jungle. The most famous swimmer-turned-actor was Johnny Weissmuller. He was born in Romania to German parents, but swam for the USA after moving there in 1908. The first man to swim the 100 metres in less than one minute, Johnny won five Olympic gold medals, setting Games records in the 100 metres freestyle event in both 1924 and 1928. He was also the star of twelve Tarzan films!

The greatest of them have won gold again and again. Denmark's Paul Elvstrom was champion in the yachting competition (**Finn class**) at every Games from 1948 to 1960. At the 1972 Games in Munich, swimmer Mark Spitz of the USA won seven gold medals – more than anyone else at a single Games – and he broke the world record seven times! Russian Vyacheslav Ivanov rowed to victory in the **single sculls** in 1956, 1960 and 1964. At the 1956 Games in Melbourne, Australia, he accidentally dropped his medal in the rowing lake while celebrating his triumph, and lost it forever. The greatest repeat-winner of all time has to be British rower Sir Steve Redgrave. Between 1984 and 2000 he was an Olympic gold-medallist a record-breaking five times.

THEN AND NOW

A long Olympic career

Britain's Thomas Thornycroft won two motor boating gold medals at the London Games of 1908. This sport never figured again at the Olympics, but Thornycroft was chosen as a reserve for Britain's yachting team forty-four years later at the 1952 Games in Helsinki. He was 70 years old at the time!

Paul Elvstrom, pictured in 1948.

OLYMPIC TEAM SPORTS

There were no team sports at the ancient Olympics. Some sports fans feel they do not belong in the modern Olympics either. The Games are meant to bring nations together in peace. But when teams rather than individuals from countries unfriendly for other reasons compete at sport, it is more likely that arguments will break out. At the 1956 Games in Melbourne, for example, the water polo final between teams from Hungary and the Soviet Union turned into a fight and had to be ended early.

GREAT OLYMPIC EVENTS

Hats off to the Hungarians

Football has been an Olympic sport since 1900. For many years **professionals** were not allowed to play, so the world's best teams seldom took the gold medal. Then at the 1952 Games in Helsinki, Hungary won every one of their Olympic matches, scoring twenty goals and letting in just two. In the four years after May 1950 Hungary did not lose a single soccer match.

WORDS TO REMEMBER

The Olympic Games are not competitions between nations. That is one of the IOC's rules, and until 1908 all athletes entered the Olympics as individuals — they were not chosen as members of teams from their home countries. But at each Games, people in the **media** count up how many medals each national team has won. Then they make a table showing which is the top Olympic country. Only five nations have ever topped this unofficial table: the Americans, Russians, British, French and Germans. The all-time winners are the Americans.

The Cuban baseball team celebrate with the Cuban flag after beating Japan in the baseball final at the 1996 Games in Atlanta.

A sledge hockey match at the 2002 Winter Olympics.

Sometimes, however, teams from unfriendly nations play even harder and produce fantastic contests. At the 1972 Games in Munich, the Russians scored in the last second of the basketball final to beat their arch-rivals the Americans by 51 points to 50. History has also shown that some teams are just bad losers whoever they play against. In 1972, the Germans won the men's hockey final against Pakistan. The Pakistanis threw water over an official and refused to face the German flag when the German anthem was played. The whole Pakistani team were banned from the Olympics for life, but the **IOC** soon relented and let them take part in the very next Games!

STRANGE BUT TRUE

Olympic rugby champions

The last winner of the Olympic rugby gold medal was the USA. That was back at the 1924 Games. France, the host country, was expected to win easily. But after they lost 17–3 to the USA, the home crowd booed and hissed so loudly that the American national anthem could not be heard. The sport was then dropped from the Olympics, and it is hardly played at all now in the USA.

The men's water polo event at the 2000 Games in Sydney.

OLYMPIC GYMNASTICS

A rhythmic gymnast demonstrates her skills.

Gymnastics were very popular in ancient Greece and Rome. They became popular again during the 1700s in Germany, where most of the **apparatus** for modern gymnastics was invented. Men have competed at Olympic gymnastic events ever since the 1896 Games in Athens, and since 1900 there has always been an all-round champion. This is the athlete with the best total score in several different exercises. These now include floor exercises and work on horizontal and parallel bars. In 1900 they included lifting a 50 kilogram stone and climbing a rope! A team event for women gymnasts was introduced at the 1928 Games in Amsterdam, Holland. Then, at Helsinki in 1952, women started to compete as individuals.

The Romanian gymnast Nadia Comaneci.

GREAT OLYMPIANS

OLGA KORBUT

At the Munich Games of 1972, everyone's eyes were on the athlete who came only seventh in the women's all-around event. She was Olga Korbut of the **Soviet Union** – seventeen years old, 150 centimetres high and weighing just 39 kilograms. Many gymnasts concentrated so hard, they seemed to perform in a trance. Tiny Olga stood out for her cheeky smile and sense of fun, which won her millions of TV fans. She went on to win gold performing floor exercises and on the balance beam.

Hockey players win gold by scoring goals; **track** athletes win by reaching the finishing line first but champion gymnasts must score the most points for their performances to get the top prize from six international judges who watch their every move. The highest possible starting score is ten. Points, or fractions of a point, are then taken away each time the gymnast makes a mistake. So everything depends on what the judges think.

Japan's Sawao Kato in action on the parallel bars at the 1976 Games in Montreal.

WORDS TO REMEMBER

PERFECT TEN

Until the 1976 Games in Montreal, no gymnast ever scored a perfect ten out of ten. Then a 14-year-old from Romania, Nadia Comaneci, achieved this feat no fewer than seven times. Her closest rival for the all-around gold medal, Nelli Kim of the Soviet Union, also top-scored twice. The electronic scoreboard could not cope. The highest score it was able to show was 9.95 – so it just flashed 1.00! Soon after those Games, 8-year-old American Mary Lou Retton scored a 1.00 in her first competition. Thinking it was meant to be a 10.00, she jumped for joy. But this time the scoreboard was correct – she really had scored just 1.00. Undeterred, Mary Lou Retton battled on and at the 1984 Games in Los Angeles, she scored some real perfect tens to win Olympic gold.

GREAT OLYMPIC EVENTS

Women's Team Combined Exercises

After the end of World War II in 1945, gymnastics became a top sport in eastern Europe. No country produced more champion gymnasts than the Soviet Union. In all ten Olympics that it entered, from Helsinki in 1952 until Barcelona in 1996, a Soviet women's team won gold in the Combined Exercises. In the same period a Soviet men's team won gold five times, the same number of times as the brilliant teams from Japan.

OLYMPIC POWER AND PRECISION

Many of the world's strongest men and women compete at Olympic combat sports and weightlifting. Some win even greater fame afterwards. Muhammad Ali, Teofilo Stevenson and Evander Holyfield all went on to become **professional** world boxing champions. The weightlifter Harold Sakata became an international star as Oddjob in the James Bond film *Goldfinger* (1964).

Iran's Hossein Rezazadeh on his way to a weightlifting gold medal at the 2000 Games in Sydney.

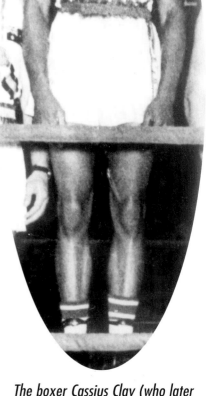

The boxer Cassius Clay (who later changed his name to Muhammad Ali) wins the light heavyweight crown at the 1960 Games in Rome.

STRANGE BUT TRUE
Winner by his Weight

At the 1956 Games in Melbourne, two weightlifters tied for first place in the super heavyweight event. Both Humberto Selvetti of Argentina and Paul Anderson of the USA lifted a total of exactly 500 kilograms. This gave them a new Olympic record to share, but who was to get the gold medal? The answer was Anderson, because his own bodyweight was 5.6 kilograms less than Selvetti's. Luckily for him, to get into shape for the Games, Anderson had made himself lose more than 25 kilograms!

WORDS TO REMEMBER

Boris 'Dis-Onishenko'

*At the 1976 Games in Montreal, experts expected the team from the **Soviet Union** to win the modern pentathlon. But they were disqualified when army major Boris Onishenko was found cheating at fencing. Fencers are wired up electrically, so when a sword tip touches an opponent to score a hit, a light goes on. Onishenko had fixed his weapon so that he could make the light come on just by pressing a button. For this piece of dishonesty, the media quickly gave him a new name: 'Dis-Onishenko'!*

The Olympic motto is swifter, higher, stronger. You might add 'more accurate' for the **precision** sports of archery, fencing, shooting and the only sport in which men and women still compete together – horse-riding. Competitors in the five events of the modern **pentathlon** have to be precise and powerful. This sport is based on the idea of a soldier who must deliver a message. Starting out on horseback (riding), he fights a duel (fencing), then has to escape a trap (shooting), cross a river (swimming) and reach his destination through a wood (cross-country running).

SWIFTER, HIGHER, STRONGER

Chris Boardman's super cycle

*Power and precision came together at the 1992 Games in Barcelona. That was when Britain's Chris Boardman showed the world his startling new cycle for the 4000 metres individual pursuit event. Specially built by the Lotus Engineering Company, it weighed only about 9 kilograms. With its one-piece **aerodynamic** frame and 3-spoke front wheel, it looked like something from a science-fiction film! Boardman broke the world record on it twice before the final, then easily won the gold medal. Some said anyone could have won on such a bike, but sporting German silver medallist Jens Lehmann said he was beaten by the man, not the machine.*

Chris Boardman at the 1992 Games in Barcelona.

TRUE OLYMPIC SPIRIT

The boxing legend Muhammad Ali lights the Olympic flame at the 1996 Games in Atlanta.

Since 1896 there have been 27 scheduled Summer Games. Athens 2004 will be the 28th. There have also been nineteen Winter Games and eleven Paralympic Games. Tens of thousands of athletes have competed for Olympic gold, but the modern Games are not meant to be all about winning. Remember those famous words from almost 100 years ago? 'The most important thing in the Olympic Games is not to win but to take part.' Win or lose, every single athlete is expected to compete with the true Olympic spirit.

WORDS TO REMEMBER

'Thanks, King'

At the 1912 Games in Stockholm, Sweden, the same athlete won the gold medal in both the pentathlon and the decathlon. This fabulous all-rounder was the USA's Jim Thorpe, who was part-Native American, part-French, part-Irish. King Gustav V of Sweden said to him, 'Sir, you are the greatest athlete in the world.' The shy Thorpe replied, 'Thanks, King.'

SWIFTER, HIGHER, STRONGER ... KINDER

The winner of the 10 kilometres (6.25 miles) cross-country skiing gold medal at the 1992 Winter Olympics in Albertville was Norway's Vegard Ulvang. The event took place during a heavy fall of snow. Ulvang's coaches advised him to wax his skis to cope with the conditions. But another competitor, Ebbe Hartz of Denmark, showed the true Olympic spirit and told him it would be better not to do this. Ulvang took Hartz's advice and went on to beat him!

No one showed this spirit better than Luz Long in 1936. The Games that year were held in Berlin, capital of Germany, Luz Long's homeland. Germany's **racist** rulers, led by Adolf Hitler, claimed that its athletes were superior to all others, especially blacks. In the long jump, Long had to compete against the black American Jesse Owens, who was having trouble with his run-up. Long, who hated racism, gave him a hint on how to sort it out. Owens powered on to take the gold. Long himself won only the silver medal, but he had gained a new friend for the rest of his life. Like so many other men and women in this book we remember him not just as a great athlete but as a great Olympian.

Luz Long (left) and Jesse Owens (right)

GREAT OLYMPIANS

The Flying Finn

Finland has a great Olympic history. Between 1912 and 1936 Finnish track athletes won 24 gold medals. No fewer than nine of them were won by Paavo Nurmi, a brilliant long-distance runner who set 29 world records between 1920 and 1928. In 1952, the Games were held in Helsinki, Finland. At the opening ceremony, an unnamed athlete entered the Olympic stadium carrying the torch. The many Finnish people in the crowd recognized his famous running style and broke into thunderous clapping. It was the great Flying Finn, Paavo Nurmi, then 55 years of age.

The Aboriginal-Australian athlete Cathy Freeman takes gold in the 400 metres at the 2000 Games in Sydney. Historically, the Aboriginal people had been persecuted by European settlers in Australia, so Freeman's triumph was a proud moment for her and her people.

OLYMPIC TIME LINE

Here is where all the Summer Games have been held.

HOST COUNTRY	MALE COMPETITORS	FEMALE COMPETITORS	NATIONS PARTICIPATING	NO. OF EVENTS
1896 Athens, Greece	311	0	14	43
1900 Paris, France	1206	19	26	87
1904 St Louis, USA	681	6	13	94
1908 London, Britain	1999	36	22	109
1912 Stockholm, Sweden	2490	57	28	102
1916 GAMES CANCELLED DURING WORLD WAR				
1920 Antwerp, Belgium	2591	78	29	154
1924 Paris, France	2956	136	44	126
1928 Amsterdam, Holland	2724	290	46	109
1932 Los Angeles, USA	1281	27	37	116
1936 Berlin, Germany	3738	328	49	129
1940 GAMES CANCELLED DURING WORLD WAR				
1944 GAMES CANCELLED DURING WORLD WAR				
1948 London, Britain	3714	385	59	136
1952 Helsinki, Finland	4407	518	69	149
1956 Melbourne, Australia	2958	384	72	151
1960 Rome, Italy	4738	610	83	50
1964 Tokyo, Japan	4457	683	93	163
1968 Mexico City, Mexico	4750	781	112	172
1972 Munich, (West) Germany	6065	1058	121	195
1976 Montreal, Canada	4781	1247	92	198
1980 Moscow, Soviet Union	4092	125	80	203
1984 Los Angeles, USA	5230	1567	140	221
1988 Seoul, South Korea	6279	2186	159	237
1992 Barcelona, Spain	6659	2708	169	257
1996 Atlanta, USA	6797	3513	197	271
2000 Sydney, Australia	6582	4069	199	300
2004 Athens, Greece	6600 (est)	5980 (est)	199 (est)	301

ADDITIONAL FACTS AND FIGURES

* How good were ancient Olympians compared to modern ones? Records survive of Protesilaus, an ancient Greek, throwing the discus 46 metres. Robert Garrett (USA) won the event at the 1896 Games in Athens with a throw of 29.15 metres. At the 1988 Games in Seoul, German Jurgen Schult won gold with a throw of 68.82 metres.

* Who has won the most Olympic medals? Gymnast Larisa Latynina (Soviet Union), who won eighteen between 1956 and 1964.

* Who is the oldest Olympic medallist? Oscar Swahn of Sweden's shooting team, who competed aged almost 73 at the 1920 Games in Antwerp.

* Which country has had the longest winning streak in a single Olympic event? The USA, whose athletes won the pole vault at every games from 1896 to 1968.

* What is the longest time between winning performances by the same athlete? Hungarian fencer Aladar Gerevich, who won Olympic gold in 1932 and then again in 1960, a gap of 28 years between medals.

HERE IS WHERE ALL THE WINTER GAMES HAVE BEEN HELD:

1924 CHAMONIX, FRANCE

1928 ST MORITZ, SWITZERLAND

1932 LAKE PLACID, USA

1936 GARMISCH-PARTENKIRCHEN, GERMANY

1948 ST MORITZ, SWITZERLAND

1952 OSLO, NORWAY

1956 CORTINA, ITALY

1960 SQUAW VALLEY, USA

1964 INNSBRUCK, AUSTRIA

1968 GRENOBLE, FRANCE

1972 SAPPORO, JAPAN

1976 INNSBRUCK, AUSTRIA

1980 LAKE PLACID, USA

1984 SARAJEVO, YUGOSLAVIA

1988 CALGARY, CANADA

1992 ALBERTVILLE, FRANCE

1994 LILLEHAMMER, NORWAY

1998 NAGANO, JAPAN

2002 SALT LAKE CITY, USA

2006 TURIN, ITALY

GLOSSARY

AD *Anno Domini (after the birth of Christ)*

aerodynamic *something designed to reduce wind resistance*

aluminium *lightweight but very strong metal*

amateur *athlete who does not compete for money*

apparatus *equipment used to perform on in gymnastic events*

BC *before Christ*

bid *process by which a country registers its interest to host an Olympics*

cox *helmsman of a ship's boat or a racing crew*

decathlon *athletic contest usually limited to men in which each contestant participates in the following ten track and field events: the 100 metres, 400 metres and 1500 metres runs; the 110 metre high hurdles; the discus and javelin throws; the shot put; the pole vault; the high jump and the long jump*

doping *process of testing an athlete to see if they have been using drugs*

fibreglass *strong, lightweight material made up of glass fibres*

field event *throwing or jumping event*

Finn class *Olympic yachting competition*

freestyle *swimming event or leg of an event in which the contestants may choose any stroke*

global *something popular all over the world*

IOC *International Olympic Committee, the body in charge of organizing the Games*

media *journalists from newspaper, television, radio and other forms of mass communication*

pentathlon *modern athletic contest, now generally limited to women's competition, in which each participant competes in five track and field events: usually the 200 metres and 1500 metres, the long jump and the discus and javelin throws*

precision *term used to refer to a sport that requires a great deal of accuracy*

professional *somebody who earns their living competing in a sport*

pursuit *event where you chase a competitor in front of you*

racist *someone who discrimates or prejudices because of a person's colour*

single sculls *very small, light racing boats*

Soviet Union *former communist country in eastern Europe and northern Asia, established in 1922. It included Russia and fourteen other Soviet Socialist Republics. Officially broke up 31 December 1991.*

sponsors *businesses that give money to an organization in return for publicity*

taxes *contribution paid by people to the government*

track event *event that takes place on the racing track inside the stadium*

unofficial *not officially sanctioned or recognized*

venues *large place where meetings (often sporting) are held*

FURTHER INFORMATION

The Olympic Spirit, Norman Barrett (Wayland, 1995)

The Olympians - A Century of Gold, Sebastian Coe with Nicholas Mason (Pavilion, 1996)

Chronicle of the Olympics, Imanu Baraka (Dorling Kindersley, 1998)

The Olympics, Neil Duncanson (Wayland, 1991)

Modern Olympic Games, Great Olympic Moments, Crises at the Olympics,
all Haydn Middleton (Heinemann Library, 1999)

www.olympic.org

www.athens.olympics.org

INDEX

A

Abrahams, Harold 14
Albertville, 1992 26
Ali, Muhammad 24, 26
Amsterdam, 1928 15, 22
ancient Olympic Games 4, 5, 9, 20, 29
Anderson, Paul 24
Antwerp, 1920 9, 13
Athens
    1896 4, 5, 10, 18, 22, 29
    2004 4, 12, 13, 26
Atlanta, 1996 10, 12, 13, 14, 26

B

Bailey, Donovan 14
Barcelona, 1992 15, 25
Beamon, Bob 17
Berlin, 1936 10, 11, 18, 27
Bikila, Abebe 5
Blankers-Koen, Fanny 14
Boardman, Chris 25
Burke, Thomas 14

C

Chamonix, 1924 7
Comaneci, Nadia 22, 23
Coubertin, Baron Pierre de 4, 5, 9
cross-country running 15, 25

D

decathlon 16
discus 16, 17, 29

E

Elvstrom, Paul 19
Ewry, Ray 16

F

fencing 25, 29
field events 16-17
Fraser, Dawn 18
Froelander, Lars 9
Freeman, Cathy 27

G

Garrett, Robert 29
Gerevich, Aladar 29
Gestring, Marjorie 18
gymnastics 22-3

H

Hajos, Alfred 18
Hansen, Connie 7
Hartz, Ebbe 26
Hary, Armin 14
Hayes, Robert 14
Helsinki, 1952 14, 22
Hines, James 14
Holyfield, Evander 24
Huegill, Geoff 9

I

IOC (International Olympic Committee) 4, 11, 13, 20, 21
Ivanov, Vyacheslav 19

J

javelin 16, 17
Johnson, Ben 13
Johnson, Michael 14
jumping 16, 17, 27

K

Keino, Kipchoge 14
Kim, Nelli 23
Klim, Michael 9
Korbut, Olga 22

L

Latynina, Larisa 29
Lehmann, Jens 25
Lewis, Carl 14
London
    1908 19
    1948 14
Long, Luz 27
Los Angeles
    1932 13
    1984 8, 16, 23, 24

M

marathon 4, 5, 7, 15
Melbourne, 1956 20, 24
Mexico, 1968 14, 17
Meyfarth, Ulrike 17
Montreal, 1976 8, 10, 23, 25
Moscow, 1980 10, 16
Munich, 1972 10, 12, 13, 17, 19, 21, 22

N

Nurmi, Paavo 15, 27

O

Olympic Games
    ceremonies and symbols 6, 8-9, 12, 25, 26
    locations 10, 11, 12, 13, 28, 29
    organization 6, 10, 12, 13, 15
Olympic villages 13
Onishenko, Boris 25
Owens, Jesse 14, 27

P

Paralympic Games 6, 7, 14, 26
Paris
    1900 18
    1924 7, 15, 21
pole vault 16, 17, 29
power and precision sports 24-5
Protesilaus 29

R

Rezazadeh, Hossein 24
Redgrave, Sir Steve 19
Retton, Mary Lou 23
Rogge, Jacques 11
Rome, 1960 5, 7

S

Sakata, Harold 24
Salt Lake City, 2002 7
Saneyev, Viktor 17
Schult, Jurgen 29
Selvetti, Humberto 24
Seoul, 1988 7, 13, 29
Shuwei, Sun 18
Spitz, Mark 19
Stevenson, Teofilo 24
Stockholm, 1912 26
Swahn, Oscar 29
swimming 9, 18, 25
Sydney, 2000 6, 8, 9, 11, 12, 14, 16, 21, 27

T

team sports 20-1
Thomson, Daley 16
Thornycroft, Thomas 19
Thorpe, Jim 26
track events 14-15, 23
Tulu, Derartu 15

U

Ulvang, Vegard 26

W

WADA (World Anti-Doping Agency) 13
water polo 20, 21
water sports 18-19
weightlifting 24
Weissmuller, Johnny 18
Winter Games 6, 11, 26, 29
women 5, 13, 15, 16, 22, 23

Z

Zatopek, Emil 14
Zatopkova, Dana 16